Amazon Transcribe Developer Guide

A catalogue record for this book is available from the Hong Kong Public Libraries.

Published in Hong Kong by Samurai Media Limited.

Email: info@samuraimedia.org

ISBN 9789888408443

Contents

What Is Amazon Transcribe?   **6**
Recognizing Voices 6
Custom Vocabulary 6
Are You a First-time User of Amazon Transcribe ? 6

How Amazon Transcribe Works   **7**
Speech Input 7
Identifying Speakers 7
Custom Vocabularies 8
Output JSON 8

Create a Custom Vocabulary   **10**
Create a Custom Vocabulary 10
    Creating a Custom Vocabulary with a Text File (Console) 10
    Creating a Custom Vocabulary with a Comma-separated Values File (Console) 10
English Character Set 11
Spanish Character Set 11

Getting Started with Amazon Transcribe   **12**

Step 1: Set up an AWS Account and Create an Administrator User   **13**
Sign up for AWS 13
Create an IAM User 13
Next Step 14

Step 2: Set up the AWS Command Line Interface (AWS CLI)   **15**
Next Step 15

Step 3: Getting Started Using the Console   **16**
Create a Transcription Job 16
View a Transcription Job 17

Step 4: Getting Started Using the API   **20**

Getting Started (AWS Command Line Interface)   **21**

Getting Started (AWS SDK for Python (Boto))   **24**

Authentication and Access Control for Amazon Transcribe   **26**
Authentication 26
Access Control 27

Overview of Managing Access Permissions to Amazon Transcribe Resources   **28**
Managing Access to Actions 28
    Identity-Based Policies (IAM Policies) 28
    Resource-Based Policies 29
Specifying Policy Elements: Resources, Actions, Effects, and Principals 29
Specifying Conditions in a Policy 29

Using Identity-based Polices (IAM Policies) for Amazon Transcribe   **30**
Permissions Required to Use the Amazon Transcribe Console 30
AWS Managed (Predefined) Polices for Amazon Transcribe 31
Permissions Required for IAM User Roles 31

Permissions Required for Amazon S3 Encryption Keys 32

Amazon Transcribe API Permissions: Actions, Resources, and Conditions Reference   **33**

Guidelines and Limits   **34**

   Supported Regions 34

   Throttling 34

   Guidelines 34

   Limits 34

Document History for Amazon Transcribe   **35**

API Reference   **36**

Actions   **37**

CreateVocabulary   **38**

   Request Syntax 38

   Request Parameters 38

   Response Syntax 38

   Response Elements 38

   Errors 39

   See Also 39

DeleteVocabulary   **40**

   Request Syntax 40

   Request Parameters 40

   Response Elements 40

   Errors 40

   See Also 40

GetTranscriptionJob   **42**

   Request Syntax 42

   Request Parameters 42

   Response Syntax 42

   Response Elements 43

   Errors 43

   See Also 43

GetVocabulary   **45**

   Request Syntax 45

   Request Parameters 45

   Response Syntax 45

   Response Elements 45

   Errors 46

   See Also 46

ListTranscriptionJobs   **47**

   Request Syntax 47

   Request Parameters 47

   Response Syntax 47

   Response Elements 48

   Errors 48

   See Also 48

ListVocabularies   **50**

Request Syntax 50
Request Parameters 50
Response Syntax 50
Response Elements 51
Errors 51
See Also 51

StartTranscriptionJob   **53**
Request Syntax 53
Request Parameters 53
Response Syntax 54
Response Elements 54
Errors 54
See Also 55

UpdateVocabulary   **56**
Request Syntax 56
Request Parameters 56
Response Syntax 56
Response Elements 56
Errors 57
See Also 57

Data Types   **58**

Media   **59**
Contents 59
See Also 59

Settings   **60**
Contents 60
See Also 60

Transcript   **61**
Contents 61
See Also 61

TranscriptionJob   **62**
Contents 62
See Also 63

TranscriptionJobSummary   **64**
Contents 64
See Also 64

VocabularyInfo   **65**
Contents 65
See Also 65

Common Errors   **66**

Common Parameters   **67**

AWS Glossary   **69**

What Is Amazon Transcribe?

Amazon Transcribe uses advanced machine learning technologies to recognize speech in audio files and transcribe them into text. You can use Amazon Transcribe to convert English and Spanish audio to text and to create applications that incorporate the content of audio files. For example, you can transcribe the audio track from a video recording to create closed captioning for the video.

You can use Amazon Transcribe with other AWS services to create applications. For example, you can:

- Use Amazon Transcribe to convert voice to text, send the text to Amazon Translate to translate it into another language, and send the translated text to Amazon Polly to speak the translated text.

- Use Amazon Transcribe to transcribe recordings of customer service calls for analysis. After transcribing a recording, send the transcription to Amazon Comprehend to identify keywords, topics, or sentiments.

Recognizing Voices

Amazon Transcribe can identify the individual speakers in an audio clip, a technique known as *diarization* or *speaker identification*. When you activate speaker identification, Amazon Transcribe includes an attribute that identifies each speaker in the audio clip. You can use speaker identification to:

- identify the customer and the support representative in a recorded customer support call
- identify characters for closed captions
- identify the speaker and questioners in a recorded press conference or lecture

You can specify the number of voices that you want Amazon Transcribe to recognize in an audio clip

Custom Vocabulary

Create a custom vocabulary to help Amazon Transcribe recognize words that are specific to your use case and improve its accuracy in converting speech to text. For example, you might create a custom vocabulary that includes industry-specific words and phrases.

Use a custom vocabulary to help Amazon Transcribe recognize:

- words that are not being recognized
- unfamiliar words that are specific to your domain

For more information about creating a custom vocabulary, see Custom Vocabularies.

Are You a First-time User of Amazon Transcribe ?

If you are a first-time user, we recommend that you read the following sections in order:

1. How Amazon Transcribe Works—Introduces Amazon Transcribe.

2. Getting Started with Amazon Transcribe—Explains how to set up your AWS account and use Amazon Transcribe.

3. API Reference—Contains reference documentation for Amazon Transcribe operations.

How Amazon Transcribe Works

Amazon Transcribe analyzes audio files that contain speech and uses advanced machine learning techniques to transcribe the voice data into text. You can then use the transcription as you would any text document.

To transcribe an audio file, Amazon Transcribe uses three operations:

- StartTranscriptionJob—Starts an asynchronous job to transcribe the speech in an audio file to text.
- ListTranscriptionJobs – Returns a list of transcription jobs that have been started. You can specify the status of the jobs that you want the operation to return. For example, you can get a list of all pending jobs, or a list of completed jobs.
- GetTranscriptionJob – Returns the result of a transcription job. The response contains a link to a JSON file containing the results.

You can also use the Amazon Transcribe to create and manage custom vocabularies for your solution. A custom vocabulary gives Amazon Transcribe more information about how to process speech in an audio clip.

- CreateVocabulary – Creates a custom vocabulary that you can use in your transcription jobs.
- DeleteVocabulary – Deletes a custom vocabulary from your account.
- GetVocabulary – Gets information about a custom vocabulary and a URL that you can use to download the contents of a vocabulary.
- ListVocabularies – Gets a list of custom vocabularies in your account.
- UpdateVocabulary – Updates an existing vocabulary.

You can use Amazon Transcribe to convert English and Spanish audio to text. You can use Amazon Translate to translate the text into another language, and use Amazon Polly to speak the text.

Speech Input

To transcribe an audio file, you use a transcription job. You store the file as an object in an Amazon S3 bucket. The input file must be:

- In FLAC, MP3, MP4, or WAV file format
- Less than 2 hours in length

You must specify the language and format of the input file.

For best results:

- Use a lossless format, such as FLAC or WAV, with PCM 16-bit encoding.
- Use a sample rate of 8000 Hz for low-fidelity audio and 16000 Hz for high-fidelity audio.

Identifying Speakers

You can have Amazon Transcribe identify the different speakers in an audio clip, a process known as *diarization* or *speaker identification*. When you enable speaker identification, Amazon Transcribe labels each fragment with the speaker that it identified.

You can specify that Amazon Transcribe identify between 2 and 10 speakers in the audio clip. You get the best performance when the number of speakers that you ask to identify matches the number of speakers in the input audio.

To turn on speaker identification, set the `MaxSpeakerLabels` and `ShowSpeakerLabels` field of the `Settings` field when you make a call to the StartTranscriptionJob operation. You must set both fields or else Amazon Transcribe will return an exception.

Custom Vocabularies

You can give Amazon Transcribe more information about how to process speech in your input file by creating a custom vocabulary. A *custom vocabulary* is a list of specific words that you want Amazon Transcribe to recognize in your audio input. These are generally domain-specific words and phrases, words that Amazon Transcribe isn't recognizing, or non-English names.

You specify the custom vocabulary as a list. Each entry can be a single word or a phrase. You separate the words of a phrase with a hyphen (-). For example, you type **IP address** as **IP-address**. For more information about creating a custom vocabulary list, see Create a Custom Vocabulary.

To create a custom vocabulary, use the CreateVocabulary or the Amazon Transcribe console. After you submit the `CreateVocabulary` request, Amazon Transcribe processes the vocabulary. To see the processing status of the vocabulary, use the GetVocabulary operation.

To use the custom vocabulary, set the `VocabularyName` field of the `Settings` field when you make a call to the StartTranscriptionJob operation.

Output JSON

When Amazon Transcribe completes a transcription job, it creates a JSON file that contains the results and saves the file in an S3 bucket. The file is identified by a user-specific URI. Use the URI to get the results.

The following is the JSON file for a short audio file:

```
1  {
2      "jobName": "job ID",
3      "accountId": "account ID",
4      "results": {
5          "transcripts": [
6              {
7                  "transcript": " that's no answer"
8              }
9          ],
10         "items": [
11             {
12                 "start_time": "0.180",
13                 "end_time": "0.470",
14                 "alternatives": [
15                     {
16                         "confidence": 0.84,
17                         "content": "that's"
18                     }
19                 ],
20                 "type": "pronunciation"
21             },
22             {
23                 "start_time": "0.0",
24                 "end_time": "0.1",
25                 "alternatives": [
26                     {
```

```
27                        "confidence": "1.0000",
28                        "content": "no"
29                    }
30                ],
31                "type": "pronunciation"
32            },
33            {
34                "start_time": "0.1",
35                "end_time": "0.2",
36                "alternatives": [
37                    {
38                        "confidence": "1.0000",
39                        "content": "answer"
40                    }
41                ],
42                "type": "pronunciation"
43            }
44        ],
45        "speaker_labels": {
46            "speakers": 2,
47            "items": [
48                {
49                    "start_time": 0,
50                    "end_time": 0.1,
51                    "speaker": "sp_0"
52                },
53                {
54                    "start_time": 0.1,
55                    "end_time": 0.2,
56                    "speaker": "sp_1"
57                }
58            ]
59        },
60        "status": "COMPLETED"
61    }
62 }
```

Create a Custom Vocabulary

A *custom vocabulary* is a list of special words and phrases that you want Amazon Transcribe to recognize in an audio clip. Use a custom vocabulary to help Amazon Transcribe recognize words and phrases that are common in your solution's domain. For example, for a medical transcription solution, you might add the names of diseases and procedures. Or you might add non-English names, such as "Etienne".

Create a Custom Vocabulary

A custom vocabulary is a list of words that you want Amazon Transcribe to recognize. Each entry in the list is a single word or phrase. Each entry must contain:

- fewer than 256 characters
- only characters from the allowed character set

For valid character sets, see English Character Set and Spanish Character Set.

The size limit for a custom vocabulary is 50 KB.

When typing a multi-word term or phrase into the custom vocabulary, separate the words with a hyphen (-) instead of a space. For example, type the term **IP address** as **IP-address**.

Create a custom vocabulary by using the CreateVocabulary operation or the Amazon Transcribe console. If you use the Amazon Transcribe console to create a custom vocabulary, you can provide the entries in either a text file or a comma-separated values file (CSV).

Creating a Custom Vocabulary with a Text File (Console)

When you use a text file, place each word or phrase on a separate line. Save the file with the extension .txt. The following is an example input file in text format:

```
1 apple
2 bear
3 coffee-dog
4 five
5 earring
6 good-morning
7 hi
8 IPhone
9 Etienne
```

Creating a Custom Vocabulary with a Comma-separated Values File (Console)

In a comma-separated values (CSV) file, separate each word or phrase with a comma. You can put multiple entries on one line, and use line returns to break long lines. Save the file with the extension ".csv".

The following is an example input file in CSV format:

```
1 apple,bear,coffee-dog,
2 five,earring,good-morning,
3 hi,IPhone,Etienne
```

English Character Set

For English custom vocabularies, you can use the following characters:

- a - z
- A - Z
- - (hyphen)

Spanish Character Set

For Spanish custom vocabularies, you can use the following characters:

- a - z
- A - Z
- - (hyphen)

You can also use the following Unicode characters:

Code	Character	Code	Character
00C1	Á	00E1	á
00C9	É	00E9	é
00CD	Í	00ED	í
00D3	Ó	0XF3	ó
00DA	Ú	00FA	ú
00D1	Ñ	0XF1	ñ
00FC	ü		

Getting Started with Amazon Transcribe

To get started using Amazon Transcribe, set up an AWS account and create an AWS Identity and Access Management (IAM) user. To use the AWS Command Line Interface (AWS CLI), download and configure it.

- Step 1: Set up an AWS Account and Create an Administrator User
- Step 2: Set up the AWS Command Line Interface (AWS CLI)
- Step 3: Getting Started Using the Console
- Step 4: Getting Started Using the API

Step 1: Set up an AWS Account and Create an Administrator User

Before you use Amazon Transcribe for the first time, complete the following tasks:

1. Sign up for AWS
2. Create an IAM User

Sign up for AWS

When you sign up for Amazon Web Services (AWS), your AWS account is automatically signed up for all AWS services, including Amazon Transcribe. You are charged only for the services that you use.

With Amazon Transcribe, you pay only for the resources that you use. If you are a new AWS customer, you can get started with Amazon Transcribe for free. For more information, see AWS Free Usage Tier.

If you already have an AWS account, skip to the next section.

To create an AWS account

1. Open https://aws.amazon.com/, and then choose **Create an AWS Account. Note**
   This might be unavailable in your browser if you previously signed into the AWS Management Console. In that case, choose **Sign in to a different account**, and then choose **Create a new AWS account**.

2. Follow the online instructions.

   Part of the sign-up procedure involves receiving a phone call and entering a PIN using the phone keypad.

Record your AWS account ID because you'll need it for the next task.

Create an IAM User

Services in AWS, such as Amazon Transcribe, require that you provide credentials when you access them. This allows the service to determine whether you have permissions to access the service's resources.

We strongly recommend that you access AWS using AWS Identity and Access Management (IAM), not the credentials for your AWS account. To use IAM to access AWS, create an IAM user, add the user to an IAM group with administrative permissions, and then grant administrative permissions to the IAM user. You can then access AWS using a special URL and the IAM user's credentials.

The Getting Started exercises in this guide assume that you have a user with administrator privileges, `adminuser`.

To create an administrator user and sign in to the console

1. Create an administrator user called `adminuser` in your AWS account. For instructions, see Creating Your First IAM User and Administrators Group in the *IAM User Guide*.

2. Sign in to the AWS Management Console using a special URL. For more information, see How Users Sign In to Your Account in the *IAM User Guide*.

For more information about IAM, see the following:

- AWS Identity and Access Management (IAM)
- Getting Started
- IAM User Guide

Next Step

Step 2: Set up the AWS Command Line Interface (AWS CLI)

Step 2: Set up the AWS Command Line Interface (AWS CLI)

You don't need the AWS CLI to perform the steps in the Getting Started exercises. However, some of the other exercises in this guide do require it. If you prefer, you can skip this step and set up the AWS CLI later.

To set up the AWS CLI

1. Download and configure the AWS CLI. For instructions, see the following topics in the *AWS Command Line Interface User Guide*:

   - Getting Set Up with the AWS Command Line Interface

   - Configuring the AWS Command Line Interface

2. In the AWS CLI `config` file, add a named profile for the administrator user:

```
1  [profile adminuser]
2  aws_access_key_id = adminuser access key ID
3  aws_secret_access_key = adminuser secret access key
4  region = aws-region
```

   You use this profile when executing the AWS CLI commands. For more information about named profiles, see Named Profiles in the *AWS Command Line Interface User Guide*. For a list of AWS Regions, see Regions and Endpoints in the *Amazon Web Services General Reference*.

3. Verify the setup by typing the following help command at the command prompt:

```
1  aws help
```

Next Step

Step 3: Getting Started Using the Console

Step 3: Getting Started Using the Console

The easiest way to get started with Amazon Transcribe is to submit a job using the console to transcribe an audio file. If you haven't reviewed the concepts and terminology in How Amazon Transcribe Works, we recommend that you do that before proceeding.

- Create a Transcription Job
- View a Transcription Job

Create a Transcription Job

Use the Amazon Transcribe console to create a transcription job for your audio files.

1. Provide the following information:

   - **Transcription job name**—A name for the job. The name must be unique within your AWS account.

   - **Amazon S3 input URL**—The Amazon S3 location of your input audio file. The location must be in the same region as the endpoint that you are calling.

   - **Language**—Choose the language of your input file. Amazon Transcribe can transcribe English and Spanish audio files.

   - **Format**—The format of the audio file. For best results you should use a lossless format such as FLAC or WAV with PCM 16-bit encoding.

   - **Media sampling rate (Hz)**—Optional. The bit sampling rate of the audio file. Amazon Transcribe accepts sample rates between 8000 Hz and 48000 Hz. For best results, you should use 8000 Hz for low-fidelity audio and 16000 for high-fidelity audio.

   The following shows the **Create Transcription Job** filled out for a sample job.

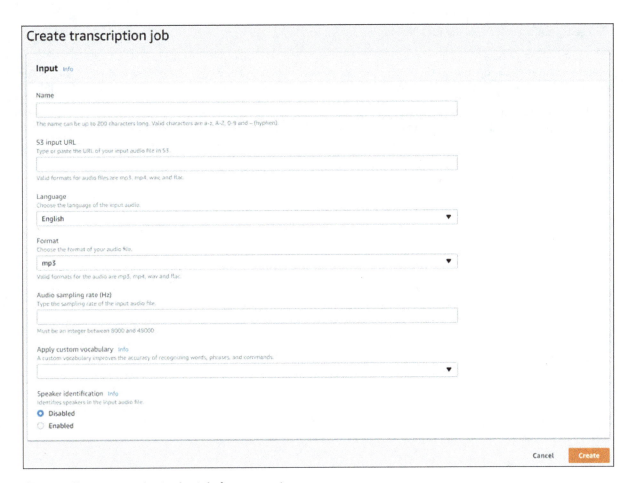

2. Choose **Create** to submit the job for processing.

View a Transcription Job

Completed transcription jobs are displayed in a list that contains a brief description of the job. The **Availability** column shows the remaining time that the job results will be kept on the server. Jobs are kept for 90 days and then deleted from the system.

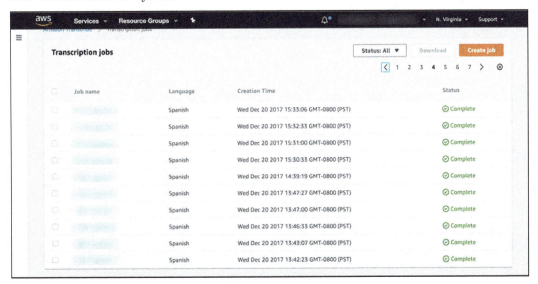

Choose a job in the list to see information about the job.

The information page about the transcription job has three sections. The **Detail** section provides details about the transcription job, including the name, information about when the job will be deleted from the server, and the input and output URLs. Use the output URL to download the output from your transcription job.

The **Output** section contains the transcription of the audio submitted to Amazon Transcribe. You can download the transcription by choosing the **Download transcription** button.

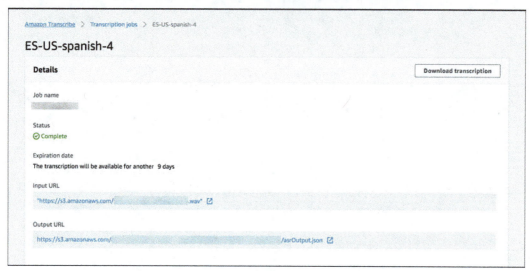

The **Code samples** section contains the JSON input for the StartTranscriptionJob operation and the output from the GetTranscriptionJob operation.

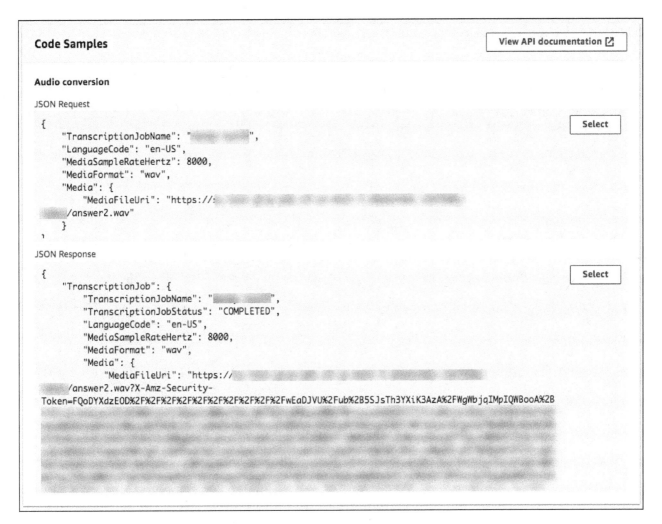

Code Samples

View API documentation ⬈

Audio conversion

JSON Request

```
{
    "TranscriptionJobName": "          ",
    "LanguageCode": "en-US",
    "MediaSampleRateHertz": 8000,
    "MediaFormat": "wav",
    "Media": {
        "MediaFileUri": "https://
        /answer2.wav"
    }
}
```

JSON Response

```
{
    "TranscriptionJob": {
        "TranscriptionJobName": "          ",
        "TranscriptionJobStatus": "COMPLETED",
        "LanguageCode": "en-US",
        "MediaSampleRateHertz": 8000,
        "MediaFormat": "wav",
        "Media": {
            "MediaFileUri": "https://
            /answer2.wav?X-Amz-Security-
Token=FQoDYXdzEOD%2F%2F%2F%2F%2F%2F%2F%2F%2F%2FwEaDJVU%2Fub%2B5SJsTh3YXiK3AzA%2FWgWbjqIMpIQWBooA%2B
```

Next Step
Step 4: Getting Started Using the API

Step 4: Getting Started Using the API

This section contains examples the demonstrate using the Amazon Transcribe API. You can use these samples to learn about the API or as building blocks in your own applications.

- Getting Started (AWS Command Line Interface)
- Getting Started (AWS SDK for Python (Boto))

Getting Started (AWS Command Line Interface)

In the following exercise, you use the AWS Command Line Interface (AWS CLI) to transcribe speech into text. To complete this exercise, you need to:

- Have a text editor.

- Be familiar with the AWS CLI. For more information, see Step 2: Set up the AWS Command Line Interface (AWS CLI).

- Have a speech file in .WAV or .MP4 format that is stored in an S3 bucket that has the proper permissions.

To transcribe text, you have to provide the input parameters in a JSON file.

To transcribe text

1. Copy your input speech to an S3 bucket. The location must be in the same region as the endpoint that you are calling. This example assumes that the file is in an S3 bucket named `test-transcribe` and that the file name is `answer2.wav`.

2. Create a JSON file named `test-start-command.json` that contains the input parameters for the Start-TranscriptionJob operation.

```
1 {
2     "TranscriptionJobName": "request ID",
3     "LanguageCode": "en-US",
4     "MediaFormat": "wav",
5     "Media": {
6         "MediaFileUri": "https://S3 endpoint/test-transcribe/answer2.wav"
7     }
8 }
```

3. In the AWS CLI, run the following command. The example is formatted for Unix, Linux, and macOS. For Windows, replace the backslash (\) Unix continuation character at the end of each line with a caret (^).

```
1 aws transcribe start-transcription-job \
2     --region region \
3     --cli-input-json file://test-start-command.json
```

Amazon Transcribe responds with the following:

```
1 {
2     "TranscriptionJob": {
3         "TranscriptionJobName": "request ID",
4         "LanguageCode": "en-US",
5         "TranscriptionJobStatus": "IN_PROGRESS",
6         "Media": {
7             "MediaFileUri": "https://S3 endpoint/test-transcribe/answer2.wav"
8         },
9         "CreationTime": timestamp,
10        "MediaFormat": "wav"
11    }
12 }
```

To list transcription jobs

- Run the following command:

```
1 aws transcribe list-transcription-jobs \
2     --region region \
3     --status IN_PROGRESS
```

Amazon Transcribe responds with the following:

```
1  {
2      "Status": "IN_PROGRESS",
3      "TranscriptionJobSummaries": [
4          {
5              "TranscriptionJobName": "request ID",
6              "LanguageCode": "en-US",
7              "CreationTime": timestamp,
8              "TranscriptionJobStatus": "IN_PROGRESS"
9          }
10     ]
11 }
```

To get the results of a transcription job

1. When the job has the status COMPLETED, get the results of the job. Type the following command:

```
1 aws transcribe get-transcription-job \
2    --region endpoint \
3    --transcription-job-name "request ID"
```

Amazon Transcribe responds with the following:

```
1  {
2      "TranscriptionJob": {
3          "TranscriptionJobName": "request ID",
4          "LanguageCode": "en-US",
5          "TranscriptionJobStatus": "COMPLETED",
6          "Media": {
7              "MediaFileUri": "input URI"
8          },
9          "CreationTime": timestamp,
10         "CompletionTime": timestamp,
11         "Transcript": {
12             "TranscriptFileUri": "output URI"
13         }
14     }
15 }
```

2. Use the output URI to get the transcribed text from the audio file. The following is the output from transcribing a short audio clip:

```
1      {
2        "jobName":"job ID",
3        "accountId":"account ID",
4        "results": {
5          "transcripts":[
6              {
7                  "transcript":" that's no answer"
8              }
9          ],
10         "items":[
11             {
12                 "start_time":"0.180",
13                 "end_time":"0.470",
14                 "alternatives":[
```

```
15          {
16              "confidence":0.84,
17              "content":"that's"
18          }
19        ],
20        "type": "pronunciation"
21      },
22      {
23        "start_time":"0.470",
24        "end_time":"0.710",
25        "alternatives":[
26          {
27              "confidence":0.99,
28              "content":"no"
29          }
30        ],
31        "type": "pronunciation"
32      },
33      {
34        "start_time":"0.710",
35        "end_time":"1.080",
36        "alternatives":[
37          {
38              "confidence":0.874,
39              "content":"answer"
40          }
41        ],
42        "type": "pronunciation"
43      }
44    ]
45  },
46  "status":"COMPLETED"
47 }
```

Getting Started (AWS SDK for Python (Boto))

In this exercise you create script that uses the SDK for Python to transcribe speech into text. To complete this exercise, you need to:

- Install the AWS CLI. For more information, see Step 2: Set up the AWS Command Line Interface (AWS CLI).

- Have a speech file in .WAV or .MP4 format that is stored in an S3 bucket that has the proper permissions. The location must be in the same region as the endpoint that you are calling. This example assumes that the file is in an Amazon S3 bucket named **test-transcribe** and that the file name is **answer2.wav**.

```python
from __future__ import print_function
import time
import boto3
transcribe = boto3.client('transcribe')
job_name = "job name"
job_uri = "https://S3 endpoint/test-transcribe/answer2.wav"
transcribe.start_transcription_job(
    TranscriptionJobName=job_name,
    Media={'MediaFileUri': job_uri},
    MediaFormat='wav',
    LanguageCode='en-US'
)
while True:
    status = transcribe.get_transcription_job(TranscriptionJobName=job_name)
    if status['TranscriptionJob']['TranscriptionJobStatus'] in ['COMPLETED', 'FAILED']:
        break
    print("Not ready yet...")
    time.sleep(5)
print(status)
```

When the transcription job is complete, the result links to an Amazon S3 presigned URL that contains the transcription in JSON format:

```json
{
    "jobName":"job ID",
    "accountId":"account ID",
    "results": {
      "transcripts":[
          {
              "transcript":" that's no answer",
              "confidence":1.0
          }
      ],
      "items":[
          {
              "start_time":"0.180",
              "end_time":"0.470",
              "alternatives":[
                  {
                      "confidence":0.84,
                      "word":"that's"
                  }
              ]
          },
```

24

```
22              {
23                  "start_time":"0.470",
24                  "end_time":"0.710",
25                  "alternatives":[
26                      {
27                          "confidence":0.99,
28                          "word":"no"
29                      }
30                  ]
31              },
32              {
33                  "start_time":"0.710",
34                  "end_time":"1.080",
35                  "alternatives":[
36                      {
37                          "confidence":0.87,
38                          "word":"answer"
39                      }
40                  ]
41              }
42          ]
43      },
44      "status":"COMPLETED"
45  }
```

Authentication and Access Control for Amazon Transcribe

Access to Amazon Transcribe requires credentials that AWS can use to authenticate your requests. Those credentials must have permissions to access Amazon Transcribe actions. The following sections provide details on how you can use AWS Identity and Access Management (IAM) and Amazon Transcribe to help secure your resources by controlling who can access them.

- Authentication
- Access Control

Authentication

You can access AWS as any of the following types of identities:

- **AWS account root user** – When you first create an AWS account, you begin with a single sign-in identity that has complete access to all AWS services and resources in the account. This identity is called the AWS account *root user* and is accessed by signing in with the email address and password that you used to create the account. We strongly recommend that you do not use the root user for your everyday tasks, even the administrative ones. Instead, adhere to the best practice of using the root user only to create your first IAM user. Then securely lock away the root user credentials and use them to perform only a few account and service management tasks.

- **IAM user** – An IAM user is an identity within your AWS account that has specific custom permissions (for example, permissions to create a custom vocabulary in Amazon Transcribe). You can use an IAM user name and password to sign in to secure AWS webpages like the AWS Management Console, AWS Discussion Forums, or the AWS Support Center.

  In addition to a user name and password, you can also generate access keys for each user. You can use these keys when you access AWS services programmatically, either through one of the several SDKs or by using the AWS Command Line Interface (CLI). The SDK and CLI tools use the access keys to cryptographically sign your request. If you don't use AWS tools, you must sign the request yourself. Amazon Transcribe supports *Signature Version 4*, a protocol for authenticating inbound API requests. For more information about authenticating requests, see Signature Version 4 Signing Process in the *AWS General Reference*.

- **IAM role** – An IAM role is an IAM identity that you can create in your account that has specific permissions. It is similar to an *IAM user*, but it is not associated with a specific person. An IAM role enables you to obtain temporary access keys that can be used to access AWS services and resources. IAM roles with temporary credentials are useful in the following situations:

  - **Federated user access** – Instead of creating an IAM user, you can use existing user identities from AWS Directory Service, your enterprise user directory, or a web identity provider. These are known as *federated users*. AWS assigns a role to a federated user when access is requested through an identity provider. For more information about federated users, see Federated Users and Roles in the *IAM User Guide*.

  - **AWS service access** – You can use an IAM role in your account to grant an AWS service permissions to access your account's resources. For example, you can create a role that allows Amazon Redshift to access an Amazon S3 bucket on your behalf and then load data from that bucket into an Amazon Redshift cluster. For more information, see Creating a Role to Delegate Permissions to an AWS Service in the *IAM User Guide*.

- **Applications running on Amazon EC2** – You can use an IAM role to manage temporary credentials for applications that are running on an EC2 instance and making AWS API requests. This is preferable to storing access keys within the EC2 instance. To assign an AWS role to an EC2 instance and make it available to all of its applications, you create an instance profile that is attached to the instance. An instance profile contains the role and enables programs that are running on the EC2 instance to get temporary credentials. For more information, see Using an IAM Role to Grant Permissions to Applications Running on Amazon EC2 Instances in the *IAM User Guide.*

Access Control

You must have valid credentials to authenticate your requests. The credentials must have permissions to call an Amazon Transcribe action.

The following sections describe how to manage permissions for Amazon Transcribe. We recommend that you read the overview first.

- Overview of Managing Access Permissions to Amazon Transcribe Resources
- Using Identity-based Polices (IAM Policies) for Amazon Transcribe

Overview of Managing Access Permissions to Amazon Transcribe Resources

Permissions to access an action are governed by permissions policies. An account administrator can attach permissions policies to IAM identities (that is, users, groups, and roles) to manage access to actions.

Note

An *account administrator* (or administrator user) is a user with administrator privileges. We strongly recommend that you access AWS using IAM not the credentials for your AWS account. To use IAM to access AWS, create an IAM user, add the user to an IAM group with administrative permissions, and then grant administrative permissions to the IAM user. You can then access AWS using a special URL and the IAM user's credentials. For more information, see IAM Best Practices in the *IAM User Guide*.

When granting permissions, you decide who is getting the permissions and the actions they get permissions for.

- Managing Access to Actions
- Specifying Policy Elements: Resources, Actions, Effects, and Principals
- Specifying Conditions in a Policy

Managing Access to Actions

A *permissions policy* describes who has access to what. You have several options for creating permissions policies.

Note

This topic discusses using IAM in the context of Amazon Transcribe. It doesn't provide detailed information about the IAM service. For complete IAM documentation, see What Is IAM? in the *IAM User Guide*. For information about IAM policy syntax and descriptions, see AWS IAM Policy Reference in the *IAM User Guide*.

Policies attached to an IAM identity are referred to as *identity-based* policies (IAM polices). Policies attached to a resource are referred to as *resource-based* policies. Amazon Transcribe supports only identity-based policies.

Identity-Based Policies (IAM Policies)

You can attach policies to IAM identities. For example, you can do the following:

- **Attach a permissions policy to a user or a group in your account**—To grant a user or a group of users permissions to call an Amazon Transcribe action, you can attach a permissions policy to a user or group that the user belongs to.

- **Attach a permissions policy to a role (grant cross-account permissions)**—To grant cross-account permissions, you can attach an identity-based permissions policy to an IAM role. For example, the administrator in Account A can create a role to grant cross-account permissions to another AWS account (for example, Account B) or an AWS service as follows:

  1. Account A administrator creates an IAM role and attaches a permissions policy to the role that grants permissions on resources in Account A.

  2. Account A administrator attaches a trust policy to the role identifying Account B as the principal who can assume the role.

  3. Account B administrator can then delegate permissions to assume the role to any users in Account B. Doing this allows users in Account B to create or access resources in Account A. If you want to grant an AWS service permissions to assume the role, the principal in the trust policy can be an AWS service principal.

  For more information about using IAM to delegate permissions, see Access Management in the *IAM User Guide*.

For more information about using identity-based policies with Amazon Transcribe, see Using Identity-based Polices (IAM Policies) for Amazon Transcribe. For more information about users, groups, roles, and permissions, see Identities (Users, Groups, and Roles) in the *IAM User Guide*.

Resource-Based Policies

Other services, such as AWS Lambda, support resource-based permissions policies. For example, you can attach a policy to an S3 bucket to manage access permissions to that bucket. Amazon Transcribe doesn't support resource-based policies.

Specifying Policy Elements: Resources, Actions, Effects, and Principals

Amazon Transcribe defines a set of API operations (see Actions). To grant permissions for these API operations, Amazon Transcribe defines a set of actions that you can specify in a policy.

The following are the most basic policy elements:

- **Resource**—In a policy, you use an Amazon Resource Name (ARN) to identify the resource to which the policy applies. For Amazon Transcribe, the resource is always *.

- **Action**—You use action keywords to identify operations that you want to allow or deny. For example, depending on the specified `Effect`, `transcribe:StartTranscriptionJob` either allows or denies the user permissions to perform the Amazon Transcribe `StartTranscriptionJob` operation.

- **Effect**—You specify the effect of the action that occurs when the user requests the specific action–this can be either allow or deny. If you don't explicitly grant access to (allow) a resource, access is implicitly denied. You can also explicitly deny access to a resource. You might do this to make sure that a user cannot access the resource, even if a different policy grants access.

- **Principal**—In identity-based policies (IAM policies), the user that the policy is attached to is the implicit principal.

To learn more about IAM policy syntax and descriptions, see AWS IAM Policy Reference in the *IAM User Guide*.

For a table of Amazon Transcribe API actions, see Amazon Transcribe API Permissions: Actions, Resources, and Conditions Reference.

Specifying Conditions in a Policy

When you grant permissions, you use the IAM policy language to specify the conditions under which a policy should take effect. For example, you might want a policy to be applied only after a specific date. For more information about specifying conditions in a policy language, see Condition in the *IAM User Guide*.

AWS provides a set of predefined condition keys for all AWS services that support IAM for access control. For example, you can use the `aws:userid` condition key to require a specific AWS ID when requesting an action. For more information and a complete list of AWS-wide keys, see Available Keys for Conditions in the *IAM User Guide*.

Note
Condition keys are case-sensitive.

Amazon Transcribe does not provide additional condition keys.

Using Identity-based Polices (IAM Policies) for Amazon Transcribe

The following identity-based policies demonstrate how an account administrator can attach permissions policies to IAM identities (users, groups, and roles) to grant permissions to perform Amazon Transcribe actions.

Important
Before you proceed, we recommend that you review Overview of Managing Access Permissions to Amazon Transcribe Resources.

The following is the permissions policy required to use the Amazon Transcribe `StartTranscriptionJob` action:

```
1  {
2      "Version": "2012-10-17",
3      "Statement": [
4          {
5              "Effect": "Allow",
6              "Action": [
7                  "transcribe:StartTranscriptionJob"
8              ],
9              "Resource": "*"
10         }
11     ]
12 }
```

The policy has one statement that grants permissions to use the `StartTranscriptionJob` action.

The policy doesn't specify the `Principal` element because you don't specify the principal who gets the permission in an identity-based policy. When you attach a policy to a user, the user is the implicit principal. When you attach a permissions policy to an IAM role, the principal identified in the role's trust policy gets the permissions.

For a table of Amazon Transcribe API actions and the resources that they apply to, see Amazon Transcribe API Permissions: Actions, Resources, and Conditions Reference.

Permissions Required to Use the Amazon Transcribe Console

To use the Amazon Transcribe console, you need to grant permissions for the actions shown in the following policy:

```
1  {
2      "Version": "2012-10-17",
3      "Statement": [
4          {
5              "Action": [
6                  "transcribe:*"
7              ],
8              "Resource": "*",
9              "Effect": "Allow"
10         }
11     ]
12 }
```

The policy enables the user to call all of the Amazon Transcribe operations.

AWS Managed (Predefined) Polices for Amazon Transcribe

AWS addresses many common use cases by providing standalone IAM policies that are created and administered by AWS. Managed policies grant necessary permissions for common use cases so you can avoid having to investigate which permissions are needed. For more information, see AWS Managed Policies in the *IAM User Guide*.

The following AWS managed polices, which you can attach to users in your account, are specific to Amazon Transcribe:

- **ReadOnly** — Grants read-only access to Amazon Transcribe resources so that you can get and list transcription jobs and custom vocabularies.

- **FullAccess** — Grants full access to create, read, update, delete, and run all Amazon Transcribe resources. It also allows access to S3 buckets with "transcribe" in the bucket name.

Note

You can review these permission policies by signing in to the IAM console and searching for specific policies.

You can also create your own custom IAM policies to allow permissions for Amazon Transcribe API actions. You can attach these custom policies to the IAM users or groups that require those permissions.

Permissions Required for IAM User Roles

When you create an IAM user to call Amazon Transcribe, the identity must have permission for the S3 bucket and to the AWS Key Management Service (AWS KMS) key used to encrypt the contents of the bucket, if you provided one.

The user must have the following IAM policy to decrypt permissions on the KMS ARN:

```
1  {
2      "Version": "2012-10-17",
3      "Statement": [
4          {
5              "Action": [
6                  "kms:Decrypt"
7              ],
8              "Resource": "KMS key ARN",
9              "Effect": "Allow"
10         }
11     ]
12 }
```

The user's IAM policy must have Amazon S3 permissions to access the S3 bucket where audio files are stored and transcriptions are saved:

```
1  {
2      "Version": "2012-10-17",
3      "Statement": [
4          {
5              "Effect": "Allow",
6              "Action": ["
7                          s3:"GetObject,
8              ],
9              "Resource": "S3 bucket location"
10         }
11     ]
12 }
```

Permissions Required for Amazon S3 Encryption Keys

If you are using an AWS Key Management Service key to encrypt an Amazon S3 bucket, include the following in the AWS KMS key policy. This allows Amazon Transcribe access to the contents of the bucket. For more information about allowing access to customer master keys, see Allowing External AWS Accounts to Access a CMK in the *AWS KMS Developer Guide*.

```
1  {
2     "Sid": "Allow-Transcribe",
3     "Effect": "Allow",
4     "Principal": {
5       "AWS": "arn:aws:iam::account id:root",
6     },
7     "Action": [
8       "kms:Decrypt"
9     ],
10    "Resource": "KMS key ARN"
11 }
```

Amazon Transcribe API Permissions: Actions, Resources, and Conditions Reference

Use the following table as a reference when setting up Access Control and writing a permissions policy that you can attach to an IAM identity (an identity-based policy). The list includes each Amazon Transcribe API operation, the corresponding action for which you can grant permissions to perform the action, and the AWS resource for which you can grant the permissions. You specify the actions in the policy's `Action` field, and you specify the resource value in the policy's `Resource` field.

To express conditions in your Amazon Transcribe policies, you can use AWS-wide condition keys. For a complete list of AWS-wide keys, see Available Keys in the *IAM User Guide*.

Note
To specify an action, use the `transcribe:` prefix followed by the API operation name, for example, `transcribe:StartTranscriptionJob`.

If you see an expand arrow () in the upper-right corner of the table, you can open the table in a new window. To close the window, choose the close button (**X**) in the lower-right corner.

Amazon Transcribe API and Required Permissions for Actions

Amazon Transcribe API Operations	Required Permissions (API Actions)	Resources
CreateVocabulary	transcribe:CreateVocabulary	*
DeleteVocabulary	transcribe:DeleteVocabulary	*
GetTranscriptionJob	transcribe:GetTranscriptionJob	*
GetVocabulary	transcribe:GetVocabulary	*
ListTranscriptionJobs	transcribe:ListTranscriptionJobs	*
ListVocabularies	transcribe:ListVocabularies	*
StartTranscriptionJob	transcribe:StartTranscriptionJob	*
UpdateVocabulary	transcribe:UpdateVocabulary	*

Guidelines and Limits

Supported Regions

For a list of AWS Regions where Amazon Transcribe is available, see AWS Regions and Endpoints in the *Amazon Web Services General Reference.*

Throttling

For information about throttling for Amazon Transcribe and to request a limit increase, see Amazon Transcribe Limits in the *Amazon Web Services General Reference.*

Guidelines

For best results:

- Use a lossless format, such as FLAC or WAV, with PCM 16-bit encoding.
- Use a sample rate of 8000 Hz for low-fidelity audio and 16000 Hz for high-fidelity audio.

Limits

Amazon Transcribe has the following limitations:

Description	Limit
Maximum audio file length	2 hours
Maximum size of a custom vocabulary	50 KB
Maximum of a custom vocabulary phrase	256 characters

Document History for Amazon Transcribe

The following table describes the documentation history for Amazon Transcribe.

- **Latest documentation update:** April 4, 2018

Change	Description	Date
New feature	Amazon Transcribe adds support for custom vocabularies. For more information, see Create a Custom Vocabulary.	April 4, 2018
New guide	This is the first release of the Amazon Transcribe Developer Guide.	November 29, 2017

API Reference

This section contains the API Reference documentation.

Actions

The following actions are supported:

- CreateVocabulary
- DeleteVocabulary
- GetTranscriptionJob
- GetVocabulary
- ListTranscriptionJobs
- ListVocabularies
- StartTranscriptionJob
- UpdateVocabulary

CreateVocabulary

Creates a new custom vocabulary that you can use to change the way Amazon Transcribe handles transcription of an audio file.

Request Syntax

```
1 {
2     "[LanguageCode](#transcribe-CreateVocabulary-request-LanguageCode)": "string",
3     "[Phrases](#transcribe-CreateVocabulary-request-Phrases)": [ "string" ],
4     "[VocabularyName](#transcribe-CreateVocabulary-request-VocabularyName)": "string"
5 }
```

Request Parameters

For information about the parameters that are common to all actions, see Common Parameters.

The request accepts the following data in JSON format.

** LanguageCode ** The language code of the vocabulary entries.
Type: String
Valid Values:en-US | es-US
Required: Yes

** Phrases ** An array of strings that contains the vocabulary entries.
Type: Array of strings
Length Constraints: Minimum length of 0. Maximum length of 256.
Required: Yes

** VocabularyName ** The name of the vocabulary. The name must be unique within an AWS account. The name is case-sensitive.
Type: String
Length Constraints: Minimum length of 1. Maximum length of 200.
Pattern: ^[0-9a-zA-Z._-]+
Required: Yes

Response Syntax

```
1 {
2     "[FailureReason](#transcribe-CreateVocabulary-response-FailureReason)": "string",
3     "[LanguageCode](#transcribe-CreateVocabulary-response-LanguageCode)": "string",
4     "[LastModifiedTime](#transcribe-CreateVocabulary-response-LastModifiedTime)": number,
5     "[VocabularyName](#transcribe-CreateVocabulary-response-VocabularyName)": "string",
6     "[VocabularyState](#transcribe-CreateVocabulary-response-VocabularyState)": "string"
7 }
```

Response Elements

If the action is successful, the service sends back an HTTP 200 response.

The following data is returned in JSON format by the service.

** FailureReason ** If the VocabularyState field is FAILED, this field contains information about why the job failed.
Type: String

** LanguageCode ** The language code of the vocabulary entries.
Type: String
Valid Values:`en-US` | `es-US`

** LastModifiedTime ** The date and time that the vocabulary was created.
Type: Timestamp

** VocabularyName ** The name of the vocabulary.
Type: String
Length Constraints: Minimum length of 1. Maximum length of 200.
Pattern: `^[0-9a-zA-Z._-]+`

** VocabularyState ** The processing state of the vocabulary. When the `VocabularyState` field contains `READY` the vocabulary is ready to be used in a `StartTranscriptionJob` request.
Type: String
Valid Values:`PENDING` | `READY` | `FAILED`

Errors

For information about the errors that are common to all actions, see Common Errors.

BadRequestException
Your request didn't pass one or more validation tests. For example, a name already exists when createing a resource or a name may not exist when getting a transcription job or custom vocabulary. See the exception `Message` field for more information.
HTTP Status Code: 400

ConflictException
The `JobName` field is a duplicate of a previously entered job name. Resend your request with a different name.
HTTP Status Code: 400

InternalFailureException
There was an internal error. Check the error message and try your request again.
HTTP Status Code: 500

LimitExceededException
Either you have sent too many requests or your input file is too long. Wait before you resend your request, or use a smaller file and resend the request.
HTTP Status Code: 400

See Also

For more information about using this API in one of the language-specific AWS SDKs, see the following:

- AWS Command Line Interface
- AWS SDK for .NET
- AWS SDK for C++
- AWS SDK for Go
- AWS SDK for Java
- AWS SDK for JavaScript
- AWS SDK for PHP V3
- AWS SDK for Python
- AWS SDK for Ruby V2

DeleteVocabulary

Deletes a vocabulary from Amazon Transcribe.

Request Syntax

```
1 {
2     "[VocabularyName](#transcribe-DeleteVocabulary-request-VocabularyName)": "string"
3 }
```

Request Parameters

For information about the parameters that are common to all actions, see Common Parameters.

The request accepts the following data in JSON format.

** VocabularyName ** The name of the vocabulary to delete.
Type: String
Length Constraints: Minimum length of 1. Maximum length of 200.
Pattern: ^[0-9a-zA-Z._-]+
Required: Yes

Response Elements

If the action is successful, the service sends back an HTTP 200 response with an empty HTTP body.

Errors

For information about the errors that are common to all actions, see Common Errors.

InternalFailureException
There was an internal error. Check the error message and try your request again.
HTTP Status Code: 500

LimitExceededException
Either you have sent too many requests or your input file is too long. Wait before you resend your request, or use a smaller file and resend the request.
HTTP Status Code: 400

NotFoundException
We can't find the requested resource. Check the name and try your request again.
HTTP Status Code: 400

See Also

For more information about using this API in one of the language-specific AWS SDKs, see the following:

- AWS Command Line Interface
- AWS SDK for .NET
- AWS SDK for C++
- AWS SDK for Go

- AWS SDK for Java
- AWS SDK for JavaScript
- AWS SDK for PHP V3
- AWS SDK for Python
- AWS SDK for Ruby V2

GetTranscriptionJob

Returns information about a transcription job. To see the status of the job, check the `TranscriptionJobStatus` field. If the status is `COMPLETED`, the job is finished and you can find the results at the location specified in the `TranscriptionFileUri` field.

Request Syntax

```
1 {
2     "[TranscriptionJobName](#transcribe-GetTranscriptionJob-request-TranscriptionJobName)": "
        string"
3 }
```

Request Parameters

For information about the parameters that are common to all actions, see Common Parameters.

The request accepts the following data in JSON format.

** TranscriptionJobName ** The name of the job.
Type: String
Length Constraints: Minimum length of 1. Maximum length of 200.
Pattern: `^[0-9a-zA-Z._-]+`
Required: Yes

Response Syntax

```
1 {
2     "[TranscriptionJob](#transcribe-GetTranscriptionJob-response-TranscriptionJob)": {
3         "[CompletionTime](API_TranscriptionJob.md#transcribe-Type-TranscriptionJob-CompletionTime)
            ": number,
4         "[CreationTime](API_TranscriptionJob.md#transcribe-Type-TranscriptionJob-CreationTime)":
            number,
5         "[FailureReason](API_TranscriptionJob.md#transcribe-Type-TranscriptionJob-FailureReason)":
            "string",
6         "[LanguageCode](API_TranscriptionJob.md#transcribe-Type-TranscriptionJob-LanguageCode)": "
            string",
7         "[Media](API_TranscriptionJob.md#transcribe-Type-TranscriptionJob-Media)": {
8             "[MediaFileUri](API_Media.md#transcribe-Type-Media-MediaFileUri)": "string"
9         },
10        "[MediaFormat](API_TranscriptionJob.md#transcribe-Type-TranscriptionJob-MediaFormat)": "
            string",
11        "[MediaSampleRateHertz](API_TranscriptionJob.md#transcribe-Type-TranscriptionJob-
            MediaSampleRateHertz)": number,
12        "[Settings](API_TranscriptionJob.md#transcribe-Type-TranscriptionJob-Settings)": {
13            "[MaxSpeakerLabels](API_Settings.md#transcribe-Type-Settings-MaxSpeakerLabels)": number
                ,
14            "[ShowSpeakerLabels](API_Settings.md#transcribe-Type-Settings-ShowSpeakerLabels)":
                boolean,
15            "[VocabularyName](API_Settings.md#transcribe-Type-Settings-VocabularyName)": "string"
16        },
17        "[Transcript](API_TranscriptionJob.md#transcribe-Type-TranscriptionJob-Transcript)": {
```

```
18        "[TranscriptFileUri](API_Transcript.md#transcribe-Type-Transcript-TranscriptFileUri)":
             "string"
19      },
20      "[TranscriptionJobName](API_TranscriptionJob.md#transcribe-Type-TranscriptionJob-
           TranscriptionJobName)": "string",
21      "[TranscriptionJobStatus](API_TranscriptionJob.md#transcribe-Type-TranscriptionJob-
           TranscriptionJobStatus)": "string"
22    }
23  }
```

Response Elements

If the action is successful, the service sends back an HTTP 200 response.

The following data is returned in JSON format by the service.

** TranscriptionJob ** An object that contains the results of the transcription job.
Type: TranscriptionJob object

Errors

For information about the errors that are common to all actions, see Common Errors.

BadRequestException
Your request didn't pass one or more validation tests. For example, a name already exists when createing a resource or a name may not exist when getting a transcription job or custom vocabulary. See the exception Message field for more information.
HTTP Status Code: 400

InternalFailureException
There was an internal error. Check the error message and try your request again.
HTTP Status Code: 500

LimitExceededException
Either you have sent too many requests or your input file is too long. Wait before you resend your request, or use a smaller file and resend the request.
HTTP Status Code: 400

NotFoundException
We can't find the requested resource. Check the name and try your request again.
HTTP Status Code: 400

See Also

For more information about using this API in one of the language-specific AWS SDKs, see the following:

- AWS Command Line Interface
- AWS SDK for .NET
- AWS SDK for C++
- AWS SDK for Go
- AWS SDK for Java
- AWS SDK for JavaScript
- AWS SDK for PHP V3

- AWS SDK for Python
- AWS SDK for Ruby V2

GetVocabulary

Gets information about a vocabulary.

Request Syntax

```
1 {
2     "[VocabularyName](#transcribe-GetVocabulary-request-VocabularyName)": "string"
3 }
```

Request Parameters

For information about the parameters that are common to all actions, see Common Parameters.

The request accepts the following data in JSON format.

** VocabularyName ** The name of the vocabulary to return information about. The name is case-sensitive.
Type: String
Length Constraints: Minimum length of 1. Maximum length of 200.
Pattern: `^[0-9a-zA-Z._-]+`
Required: Yes

Response Syntax

```
1 {
2     "[DownloadUri](#transcribe-GetVocabulary-response-DownloadUri)": "string",
3     "[FailureReason](#transcribe-GetVocabulary-response-FailureReason)": "string",
4     "[LanguageCode](#transcribe-GetVocabulary-response-LanguageCode)": "string",
5     "[LastModifiedTime](#transcribe-GetVocabulary-response-LastModifiedTime)": number,
6     "[VocabularyName](#transcribe-GetVocabulary-response-VocabularyName)": "string",
7     "[VocabularyState](#transcribe-GetVocabulary-response-VocabularyState)": "string"
8 }
```

Response Elements

If the action is successful, the service sends back an HTTP 200 response.

The following data is returned in JSON format by the service.

** DownloadUri ** The S3 location where the vocabulary is stored. Use this URI to get the contents of the vocabulary. The URI is available for a limited time.
Type: String
Length Constraints: Minimum length of 1. Maximum length of 2000.

** FailureReason ** If the `VocabularyState` field is `FAILED`, this field contains information about why the job failed.
Type: String

** LanguageCode ** The language code of the vocabulary entries.
Type: String
Valid Values:`en-US` | `es-US`

** LastModifiedTime ** The date and time that the vocabulary was last modified.
Type: Timestamp

** VocabularyName ** The name of the vocabulary to return.
Type: String
Length Constraints: Minimum length of 1. Maximum length of 200.
Pattern: `^[0-9a-zA-Z._-]+`

** VocabularyState ** The processing state of the vocabulary.
Type: String
Valid Values:`PENDING | READY | FAILED`

Errors

For information about the errors that are common to all actions, see Common Errors.

BadRequestException
Your request didn't pass one or more validation tests. For example, a name already exists when createing a resource or a name may not exist when getting a transcription job or custom vocabulary. See the exception `Message` field for more information.
HTTP Status Code: 400

InternalFailureException
There was an internal error. Check the error message and try your request again.
HTTP Status Code: 500

LimitExceededException
Either you have sent too many requests or your input file is too long. Wait before you resend your request, or use a smaller file and resend the request.
HTTP Status Code: 400

NotFoundException
We can't find the requested resource. Check the name and try your request again.
HTTP Status Code: 400

See Also

For more information about using this API in one of the language-specific AWS SDKs, see the following:

- AWS Command Line Interface
- AWS SDK for .NET
- AWS SDK for C++
- AWS SDK for Go
- AWS SDK for Java
- AWS SDK for JavaScript
- AWS SDK for PHP V3
- AWS SDK for Python
- AWS SDK for Ruby V2

ListTranscriptionJobs

Lists transcription jobs with the specified status.

Request Syntax

```
1 {
2     "[JobNameContains](#transcribe-ListTranscriptionJobs-request-JobNameContains)": "string",
3     "[MaxResults](#transcribe-ListTranscriptionJobs-request-MaxResults)": number,
4     "[NextToken](#transcribe-ListTranscriptionJobs-request-NextToken)": "string",
5     "[Status](#transcribe-ListTranscriptionJobs-request-Status)": "string"
6 }
```

Request Parameters

For information about the parameters that are common to all actions, see Common Parameters.

The request accepts the following data in JSON format.

** JobNameContains ** When specified, the jobs returned in the list are limited to jobs whose name contains the specified string.
Type: String
Length Constraints: Minimum length of 1. Maximum length of 200.
Pattern: ^[0-9a-zA-Z._-]+
Required: No

** MaxResults ** The maximum number of jobs to return in the response. If there are fewer results in the list, this response contains only the actual results.
Type: Integer
Valid Range: Minimum value of 1. Maximum value of 100.
Required: No

** NextToken ** If the result of the previous request to ListTranscriptionJobs was truncated, include the NextToken to fetch the next set of jobs.
Type: String
Length Constraints: Maximum length of 8192.
Required: No

** Status ** When specified, returns only transcription jobs with the specified status.
Type: String
Valid Values:IN_PROGRESS | FAILED | COMPLETED
Required: No

Response Syntax

```
1 {
2     "[NextToken](#transcribe-ListTranscriptionJobs-response-NextToken)": "string",
3     "[Status](#transcribe-ListTranscriptionJobs-response-Status)": "string",
4     "[TranscriptionJobSummaries](#transcribe-ListTranscriptionJobs-response-
          TranscriptionJobSummaries)": [
5         {
6             "[CompletionTime](API_TranscriptionJobSummary.md#transcribe-Type-
                  TranscriptionJobSummary-CompletionTime)": number,
```

```
7      "[CreationTime](API_TranscriptionJobSummary.md#transcribe-Type-TranscriptionJobSummary-
             CreationTime)": number,
8      "[FailureReason](API_TranscriptionJobSummary.md#transcribe-Type-TranscriptionJobSummary
             -FailureReason)": "string",
9      "[LanguageCode](API_TranscriptionJobSummary.md#transcribe-Type-TranscriptionJobSummary-
             LanguageCode)": "string",
10     "[TranscriptionJobName](API_TranscriptionJobSummary.md#transcribe-Type-
             TranscriptionJobSummary-TranscriptionJobName)": "string",
11     "[TranscriptionJobStatus](API_TranscriptionJobSummary.md#transcribe-Type-
             TranscriptionJobSummary-TranscriptionJobStatus)": "string"
12      }
13    ]
14 }
```

Response Elements

If the action is successful, the service sends back an HTTP 200 response.

The following data is returned in JSON format by the service.

** NextToken ** The `ListTranscriptionJobs` operation returns a page of jobs at a time. The maximum size of the page is set by the `MaxResults` parameter. If there are more jobs in the list than the page size, Amazon Transcribe returns the `NextPage` token. Include the token in the next request to the `ListTranscriptionJobs` operation to return in the next page of jobs.
Type: String
Length Constraints: Maximum length of 8192.

** Status ** The requested status of the jobs returned.
Type: String
Valid Values:`IN_PROGRESS | FAILED | COMPLETED`

** TranscriptionJobSummaries ** A list of objects containing summary information for a transcription job.
Type: Array of TranscriptionJobSummary objects

Errors

For information about the errors that are common to all actions, see Common Errors.

BadRequestException
Your request didn't pass one or more validation tests. For example, a name already exists when creating a resource or a name may not exist when getting a transcription job or custom vocabulary. See the exception `Message` field for more information.
HTTP Status Code: 400

InternalFailureException
There was an internal error. Check the error message and try your request again.
HTTP Status Code: 500

LimitExceededException
Either you have sent too many requests or your input file is too long. Wait before you resend your request, or use a smaller file and resend the request.
HTTP Status Code: 400

See Also

For more information about using this API in one of the language-specific AWS SDKs, see the following:

- AWS Command Line Interface
- AWS SDK for .NET
- AWS SDK for C++
- AWS SDK for Go
- AWS SDK for Java
- AWS SDK for JavaScript
- AWS SDK for PHP V3
- AWS SDK for Python
- AWS SDK for Ruby V2

ListVocabularies

Returns a list of vocabularies that match the specified criteria. If no criteria are specified, returns the entire list of vocabularies.

Request Syntax

```
1 {
2    "[MaxResults](#transcribe-ListVocabularies-request-MaxResults)": number,
3    "[NameContains](#transcribe-ListVocabularies-request-NameContains)": "string",
4    "[NextToken](#transcribe-ListVocabularies-request-NextToken)": "string",
5    "[StateEquals](#transcribe-ListVocabularies-request-StateEquals)": "string"
6 }
```

Request Parameters

For information about the parameters that are common to all actions, see Common Parameters.

The request accepts the following data in JSON format.

** MaxResults ** The maximum number of vocabularies to return in the response. If there are fewer results in the list, this response contains only the actual results.
Type: Integer
Valid Range: Minimum value of 1. Maximum value of 100.
Required: No

** NameContains ** When specified, the vocabularies returned in the list are limited to vocabularies whose name contains the specified string. The search is case-insensitive, `ListVocabularies` will return both "vocabularyname" and "VocabularyName" in the response list.
Type: String
Length Constraints: Minimum length of 1. Maximum length of 200.
Pattern: `^[0-9a-zA-Z._-]+`
Required: No

** NextToken ** If the result of the previous request to `ListVocabularies` was truncated, include the `NextToken` to fetch the next set of jobs.
Type: String
Length Constraints: Maximum length of 8192.
Required: No

** StateEquals ** When specified, only returns vocabularies with the `VocabularyState` field equal to the specified state.
Type: String
Valid Values: `PENDING | READY | FAILED`
Required: No

Response Syntax

```
1 {
2    "[NextToken](#transcribe-ListVocabularies-response-NextToken)": "string",
3    "[Status](#transcribe-ListVocabularies-response-Status)": "string",
4    "[Vocabularies](#transcribe-ListVocabularies-response-Vocabularies)": [
5       {
```

```
  6          "[LanguageCode](API_VocabularyInfo.md#transcribe-Type-VocabularyInfo-LanguageCode)": "
                 string",
  7          "[LastModifiedTime](API_VocabularyInfo.md#transcribe-Type-VocabularyInfo-
                 LastModifiedTime)": number,
  8          "[VocabularyName](API_VocabularyInfo.md#transcribe-Type-VocabularyInfo-VocabularyName)
                 ": "string",
  9          "[VocabularyState](API_VocabularyInfo.md#transcribe-Type-VocabularyInfo-VocabularyState
                 )": "string"
 10       }
 11    ]
 12 }
```

Response Elements

If the action is successful, the service sends back an HTTP 200 response.

The following data is returned in JSON format by the service.

** NextToken ** The `ListVocabularies` operation returns a page of vocabularies at a time. The maximum size of the page is set by the `MaxResults` parameter. If there are more jobs in the list than the page size, Amazon Transcribe returns the `NextPage` token. Include the token in the next request to the `ListVocabularies` operation to return in the next page of jobs.
Type: String
Length Constraints: Maximum length of 8192.

** Status ** The requested vocabulary state.
Type: String
Valid Values:`IN_PROGRESS | FAILED | COMPLETED`

** Vocabularies ** A list of objects that describe the vocabularies that match the search criteria in the request.
Type: Array of VocabularyInfo objects

Errors

For information about the errors that are common to all actions, see Common Errors.

BadRequestException
Your request didn't pass one or more validation tests. For example, a name already exists when createing a resource or a name may not exist when getting a transcription job or custom vocabulary. See the exception `Message` field for more information.
HTTP Status Code: 400

InternalFailureException
There was an internal error. Check the error message and try your request again.
HTTP Status Code: 500

LimitExceededException
Either you have sent too many requests or your input file is too long. Wait before you resend your request, or use a smaller file and resend the request.
HTTP Status Code: 400

See Also

For more information about using this API in one of the language-specific AWS SDKs, see the following:

- AWS Command Line Interface

- AWS SDK for .NET
- AWS SDK for C++
- AWS SDK for Go
- AWS SDK for Java
- AWS SDK for JavaScript
- AWS SDK for PHP V3
- AWS SDK for Python
- AWS SDK for Ruby V2

StartTranscriptionJob

Starts an asynchronous job to transcribe speech to text.

Request Syntax

```
1  {
2    "[LanguageCode](#transcribe-StartTranscriptionJob-request-LanguageCode)": "string",
3    "[Media](#transcribe-StartTranscriptionJob-request-Media)": {
4      "[MediaFileUri](API_Media.md#transcribe-Type-Media-MediaFileUri)": "string"
5    },
6    "[MediaFormat](#transcribe-StartTranscriptionJob-request-MediaFormat)": "string",
7    "[MediaSampleRateHertz](#transcribe-StartTranscriptionJob-request-MediaSampleRateHertz)":
         number,
8    "[Settings](#transcribe-StartTranscriptionJob-request-Settings)": {
9      "[MaxSpeakerLabels](API_Settings.md#transcribe-Type-Settings-MaxSpeakerLabels)": number,
10     "[ShowSpeakerLabels](API_Settings.md#transcribe-Type-Settings-ShowSpeakerLabels)": boolean
         ,
11     "[VocabularyName](API_Settings.md#transcribe-Type-Settings-VocabularyName)": "string"
12   },
13   "[TranscriptionJobName](#transcribe-StartTranscriptionJob-request-TranscriptionJobName)": "
         string"
14 }
```

Request Parameters

For information about the parameters that are common to all actions, see Common Parameters.

The request accepts the following data in JSON format.

** LanguageCode ** The language code for the language used in the input media file.
Type: String
Valid Values:en-US | es-US
Required: Yes

** Media ** An object that describes the input media for a transcription job.
Type: Media object
Required: Yes

** MediaFormat ** The format of the input media file.
Type: String
Valid Values:mp3 | mp4 | wav | flac
Required: Yes

** MediaSampleRateHertz ** The sample rate, in Hertz, of the audio track in the input media file.
Type: Integer
Valid Range: Minimum value of 8000. Maximum value of 48000.
Required: No

** Settings ** A Settings object that provides optional settings for a transcription job.
Type: Settings object
Required: No

** TranscriptionJobName ** The name of the job. The name must be unique within an AWS account.
Type: String
Length Constraints: Minimum length of 1. Maximum length of 200.

Pattern: ^[0-9a-zA-Z._-]+
Required: Yes

Response Syntax

```
1  {
2      "[TranscriptionJob](#transcribe-StartTranscriptionJob-response-TranscriptionJob)": {
3          "[CompletionTime](API_TranscriptionJob.md#transcribe-Type-TranscriptionJob-CompletionTime)
               ": number,
4          "[CreationTime](API_TranscriptionJob.md#transcribe-Type-TranscriptionJob-CreationTime)":
               number,
5          "[FailureReason](API_TranscriptionJob.md#transcribe-Type-TranscriptionJob-FailureReason)":
               "string",
6          "[LanguageCode](API_TranscriptionJob.md#transcribe-Type-TranscriptionJob-LanguageCode)": "
               string",
7          "[Media](API_TranscriptionJob.md#transcribe-Type-TranscriptionJob-Media)": {
8              "[MediaFileUri](API_Media.md#transcribe-Type-Media-MediaFileUri)": "string"
9          },
10         "[MediaFormat](API_TranscriptionJob.md#transcribe-Type-TranscriptionJob-MediaFormat)": "
               string",
11         "[MediaSampleRateHertz](API_TranscriptionJob.md#transcribe-Type-TranscriptionJob-
               MediaSampleRateHertz)": number,
12         "[Settings](API_TranscriptionJob.md#transcribe-Type-TranscriptionJob-Settings)": {
13             "[MaxSpeakerLabels](API_Settings.md#transcribe-Type-Settings-MaxSpeakerLabels)": number
                   ,
14             "[ShowSpeakerLabels](API_Settings.md#transcribe-Type-Settings-ShowSpeakerLabels)":
                   boolean,
15             "[VocabularyName](API_Settings.md#transcribe-Type-Settings-VocabularyName)": "string"
16         },
17         "[Transcript](API_TranscriptionJob.md#transcribe-Type-TranscriptionJob-Transcript)": {
18             "[TranscriptFileUri](API_Transcript.md#transcribe-Type-Transcript-TranscriptFileUri)":
                   "string"
19         },
20         "[TranscriptionJobName](API_TranscriptionJob.md#transcribe-Type-TranscriptionJob-
               TranscriptionJobName)": "string",
21         "[TranscriptionJobStatus](API_TranscriptionJob.md#transcribe-Type-TranscriptionJob-
               TranscriptionJobStatus)": "string"
22     }
23 }
```

Response Elements

If the action is successful, the service sends back an HTTP 200 response.

The following data is returned in JSON format by the service.

** TranscriptionJob ** An object containing details of the asynchronous transcription job.
Type: TranscriptionJob object

Errors

For information about the errors that are common to all actions, see Common Errors.

BadRequestException

Your request didn't pass one or more validation tests. For example, a name already exists when createing a resource or a name may not exist when getting a transcription job or custom vocabulary. See the exception `Message` field for more information.
HTTP Status Code: 400

ConflictException

The `JobName` field is a duplicate of a previously entered job name. Resend your request with a different name.
HTTP Status Code: 400

InternalFailureException

There was an internal error. Check the error message and try your request again.
HTTP Status Code: 500

LimitExceededException

Either you have sent too many requests or your input file is too long. Wait before you resend your request, or use a smaller file and resend the request.
HTTP Status Code: 400

See Also

For more information about using this API in one of the language-specific AWS SDKs, see the following:

- AWS Command Line Interface
- AWS SDK for .NET
- AWS SDK for C++
- AWS SDK for Go
- AWS SDK for Java
- AWS SDK for JavaScript
- AWS SDK for PHP V3
- AWS SDK for Python
- AWS SDK for Ruby V2

UpdateVocabulary

Updates an existing vocabulary with new values. The `UpdateVocabulary` operation overwrites all of the existing information with the values that you provide in the request.

Request Syntax

```
1 {
2    "[LanguageCode](#transcribe-UpdateVocabulary-request-LanguageCode)": "string",
3    "[Phrases](#transcribe-UpdateVocabulary-request-Phrases)": [ "string" ],
4    "[VocabularyName](#transcribe-UpdateVocabulary-request-VocabularyName)": "string"
5 }
```

Request Parameters

For information about the parameters that are common to all actions, see Common Parameters.

The request accepts the following data in JSON format.

** LanguageCode ** The language code of the vocabulary entries.
Type: String
Valid Values:`en-US` | `es-US`
Required: Yes

** Phrases ** An array of strings containing the vocabulary entries.
Type: Array of strings
Length Constraints: Minimum length of 0. Maximum length of 256.
Required: Yes

** VocabularyName ** The name of the vocabulary to update. The name is case-sensitive.
Type: String
Length Constraints: Minimum length of 1. Maximum length of 200.
Pattern: `^[0-9a-zA-Z._-]+`
Required: Yes

Response Syntax

```
1 {
2    "[LanguageCode](#transcribe-UpdateVocabulary-response-LanguageCode)": "string",
3    "[LastModifiedTime](#transcribe-UpdateVocabulary-response-LastModifiedTime)": number,
4    "[VocabularyName](#transcribe-UpdateVocabulary-response-VocabularyName)": "string",
5    "[VocabularyState](#transcribe-UpdateVocabulary-response-VocabularyState)": "string"
6 }
```

Response Elements

If the action is successful, the service sends back an HTTP 200 response.

The following data is returned in JSON format by the service.

** LanguageCode ** The language code of the vocabulary entries.
Type: String
Valid Values:`en-US` | `es-US`

** LastModifiedTime ** The date and time that the vocabulary was updated.
Type: Timestamp

** VocabularyName ** The name of the vocabulary that was updated.
Type: String
Length Constraints: Minimum length of 1. Maximum length of 200.
Pattern: `^[0-9a-zA-Z._-]+`

** VocabularyState ** The processing state of the vocabulary. When the `VocabularyState` field contains `READY` the vocabulary is ready to be used in a `StartTranscriptionJob` request.
Type: String
Valid Values:`PENDING | READY | FAILED`

Errors

For information about the errors that are common to all actions, see Common Errors.

BadRequestException
Your request didn't pass one or more validation tests. For example, a name already exists when createing a resource or a name may not exist when getting a transcription job or custom vocabulary. See the exception `Message` field for more information.
HTTP Status Code: 400

InternalFailureException
There was an internal error. Check the error message and try your request again.
HTTP Status Code: 500

LimitExceededException
Either you have sent too many requests or your input file is too long. Wait before you resend your request, or use a smaller file and resend the request.
HTTP Status Code: 400

NotFoundException
We can't find the requested resource. Check the name and try your request again.
HTTP Status Code: 400

See Also

For more information about using this API in one of the language-specific AWS SDKs, see the following:

- AWS Command Line Interface
- AWS SDK for .NET
- AWS SDK for C++
- AWS SDK for Go
- AWS SDK for Java
- AWS SDK for JavaScript
- AWS SDK for PHP V3
- AWS SDK for Python
- AWS SDK for Ruby V2

Data Types

The following data types are supported:

- Media
- Settings
- Transcript
- TranscriptionJob
- TranscriptionJobSummary
- VocabularyInfo

Media

Describes the input media file in a transcription request.

Contents

MediaFileUri The S3 location of the input media file. The URI must be in the same region as the API endpoint that you are calling. The general form is:

`https://<aws-region>.amazonaws.com/<bucket-name>/<keyprefix>/<objectkey>`

For example:

`https://s3-us-east-1.amazonaws.com/examplebucket/example.mp4`

`https://s3-us-east-1.amazonaws.com/examplebucket/mediadocs/example.mp4`

For more information about S3 object names, see Object Keys in the *Amazon S3 Developer Guide*.

Type: String

Length Constraints: Minimum length of 1. Maximum length of 2000.

Required: No

See Also

For more information about using this API in one of the language-specific AWS SDKs, see the following:

- AWS SDK for C++
- AWS SDK for Go
- AWS SDK for Java
- AWS SDK for Ruby V2

Settings

Provides optional settings for the `StartTranscriptionJob` operation.

Contents

MaxSpeakerLabels The maximum number of speakers to identify in the input audio. If there are more speakers in the audio than this number, multiple speakers will be identified as a single speaker. If you specify the `MaxSpeakerLabels` field, you must set the `ShowSpeakerLabels` field to true.
Type: Integer
Valid Range: Minimum value of 2. Maximum value of 10.
Required: No

ShowSpeakerLabels Determines whether the transcription job should use speaker recognition to identify different speakers in the input audio. If you set the `ShowSpeakerLabels` field to true, you must also set the maximum number of speaker labels `MaxSpeakerLabels` field.
Type: Boolean
Required: No

VocabularyName The name of a vocabulary to use when processing the transcription job.
Type: String
Length Constraints: Minimum length of 1. Maximum length of 200.
Pattern: `^[0-9a-zA-Z._-]+`
Required: No

See Also

For more information about using this API in one of the language-specific AWS SDKs, see the following:

- AWS SDK for C++
- AWS SDK for Go
- AWS SDK for Java
- AWS SDK for Ruby V2

Transcript

Describes the output of a transcription job.

Contents

TranscriptFileUri The S3 location where the transcription result is stored. Use this URI to access the results of the transcription job.
Type: String
Length Constraints: Minimum length of 1. Maximum length of 2000.
Required: No

See Also

For more information about using this API in one of the language-specific AWS SDKs, see the following:

- AWS SDK for C++
- AWS SDK for Go
- AWS SDK for Java
- AWS SDK for Ruby V2

TranscriptionJob

Describes an asynchronous transcription job that was created with the `StartTranscriptionJob` operation.

Contents

CompletionTime Timestamp of the date and time that the job completed.
Type: Timestamp
Required: No

CreationTime Timestamp of the date and time that the job was created.
Type: Timestamp
Required: No

FailureReason If the `TranscriptionJobStatus` field is `FAILED`, this field contains information about why the job failed.
Type: String
Required: No

LanguageCode The language code for the input speech.
Type: String
Valid Values:`en-US` | `es-US`
Required: No

Media An object that describes the input media for a transcription job.
Type: Media object
Required: No

MediaFormat The format of the input media file.
Type: String
Valid Values:`mp3` | `mp4` | `wav` | `flac`
Required: No

MediaSampleRateHertz The sample rate, in Hertz, of the audio track in the input media file.
Type: Integer
Valid Range: Minimum value of 8000. Maximum value of 48000.
Required: No

Settings Optional settings for the transcription job.
Type: Settings object
Required: No

Transcript An object that describes the output of the transcription job.
Type: Transcript object
Required: No

TranscriptionJobName A name to identify the transcription job.
Type: String
Length Constraints: Minimum length of 1. Maximum length of 200.
Pattern: `^[0-9a-zA-Z._-]+`
Required: No

TranscriptionJobStatus The status of the transcription job.
Type: String
Valid Values:`IN_PROGRESS` | `FAILED` | `COMPLETED`
Required: No

See Also

For more information about using this API in one of the language-specific AWS SDKs, see the following:

- AWS SDK for C++
- AWS SDK for Go
- AWS SDK for Java
- AWS SDK for Ruby V2

TranscriptionJobSummary

Provides a summary of information about a transcription job.

Contents

CompletionTime Timestamp of the date and time that the job completed.
Type: Timestamp
Required: No

CreationTime Timestamp of the date and time that the job was created.
Type: Timestamp
Required: No

FailureReason If the `TranscriptionJobStatus` field is `FAILED`, this field contains a description of the error.
Type: String
Required: No

LanguageCode The language code for the input speech.
Type: String
Valid Values:`en-US | es-US`
Required: No

TranscriptionJobName The name assigned to the transcription job when it was created.
Type: String
Length Constraints: Minimum length of 1. Maximum length of 200.
Pattern: `^[0-9a-zA-Z._-]+`
Required: No

TranscriptionJobStatus The status of the transcription job. When the status is `COMPLETED`, use the `GetTranscriptionJob` operation to get the results of the transcription.
Type: String
Valid Values:`IN_PROGRESS | FAILED | COMPLETED`
Required: No

See Also

For more information about using this API in one of the language-specific AWS SDKs, see the following:

- AWS SDK for C++
- AWS SDK for Go
- AWS SDK for Java
- AWS SDK for Ruby V2

VocabularyInfo

Provides information about a custom vocabulary.

Contents

LanguageCode The language code of the vocabulary entries.
Type: String
Valid Values:`en-US` | `es-US`
Required: No

LastModifiedTime The date and time that the vocabulary was last modified.
Type: Timestamp
Required: No

VocabularyName The name of the vocabulary.
Type: String
Length Constraints: Minimum length of 1. Maximum length of 200.
Pattern: `^[0-9a-zA-Z._-]+`
Required: No

VocabularyState The processing state of the vocabulary. If the state is `READY` you can use the vocabulary in a `StartTranscriptionJob` request.
Type: String
Valid Values:`PENDING` | `READY` | `FAILED`
Required: No

See Also

For more information about using this API in one of the language-specific AWS SDKs, see the following:

- AWS SDK for C++
- AWS SDK for Go
- AWS SDK for Java
- AWS SDK for Ruby V2

Common Errors

This section lists the errors common to the API actions of all AWS services. For errors specific to an API action for this service, see the topic for that API action.

AccessDeniedException
You do not have sufficient access to perform this action.
HTTP Status Code: 400

IncompleteSignature
The request signature does not conform to AWS standards.
HTTP Status Code: 400

InternalFailure The request processing has failed because of an unknown error, exception or failure.
HTTP Status Code: 500

InvalidAction The action or operation requested is invalid. Verify that the action is typed correctly.
HTTP Status Code: 400

InvalidClientTokenId The X.509 certificate or AWS access key ID provided does not exist in our records.
HTTP Status Code: 403

InvalidParameterCombination Parameters that must not be used together were used together.
HTTP Status Code: 400

InvalidParameterValue An invalid or out-of-range value was supplied for the input parameter.
HTTP Status Code: 400

InvalidQueryParameter The AWS query string is malformed or does not adhere to AWS standards.
HTTP Status Code: 400

MalformedQueryString The query string contains a syntax error.
HTTP Status Code: 404

MissingAction The request is missing an action or a required parameter.
HTTP Status Code: 400

MissingAuthenticationToken The request must contain either a valid (registered) AWS access key ID or X.509 certificate.
HTTP Status Code: 403

MissingParameter A required parameter for the specified action is not supplied.
HTTP Status Code: 400

OptInRequired The AWS access key ID needs a subscription for the service.
HTTP Status Code: 403

RequestExpired The request reached the service more than 15 minutes after the date stamp on the request or more than 15 minutes after the request expiration date (such as for pre-signed URLs), or the date stamp on the request is more than 15 minutes in the future.
HTTP Status Code: 400

ServiceUnavailable The request has failed due to a temporary failure of the server.
HTTP Status Code: 503

ThrottlingException The request was denied due to request throttling.
HTTP Status Code: 400

ValidationError The input fails to satisfy the constraints specified by an AWS service.
HTTP Status Code: 400

Common Parameters

The following list contains the parameters that all actions use for signing Signature Version 4 requests with a query string. Any action-specific parameters are listed in the topic for that action. For more information about Signature Version 4, see Signature Version 4 Signing Process in the *Amazon Web Services General Reference*.

Action The action to be performed.
Type: string
Required: Yes

Version The API version that the request is written for, expressed in the format YYYY-MM-DD.
Type: string
Required: Yes

X-Amz-Algorithm The hash algorithm that you used to create the request signature.
Condition: Specify this parameter when you include authentication information in a query string instead of in the HTTP authorization header.
Type: string
Valid Values: `AWS4-HMAC-SHA256`
Required: Conditional

X-Amz-Credential The credential scope value, which is a string that includes your access key, the date, the region you are targeting, the service you are requesting, and a termination string ("aws4_request"). The value is expressed in the following format: *access_key/YYYYMMDD/region/service*/aws4_request.
For more information, see Task 2: Create a String to Sign for Signature Version 4 in the *Amazon Web Services General Reference*.
Condition: Specify this parameter when you include authentication information in a query string instead of in the HTTP authorization header.
Type: string
Required: Conditional

X-Amz-Date The date that is used to create the signature. The format must be ISO 8601 basic format (YYYYMMDD'T'HHMMSS'Z'). For example, the following date time is a valid X-Amz-Date value: `20120325 T120000Z`.
Condition: X-Amz-Date is optional for all requests; it can be used to override the date used for signing requests. If the Date header is specified in the ISO 8601 basic format, X-Amz-Date is not required. When X-Amz-Date is used, it always overrides the value of the Date header. For more information, see Handling Dates in Signature Version 4 in the *Amazon Web Services General Reference*.
Type: string
Required: Conditional

X-Amz-Security-Token The temporary security token that was obtained through a call to AWS Security Token Service (AWS STS). For a list of services that support temporary security credentials from AWS Security Token Service, go to AWS Services That Work with IAM in the *IAM User Guide*.
Condition: If you're using temporary security credentials from the AWS Security Token Service, you must include the security token.
Type: string
Required: Conditional

X-Amz-Signature Specifies the hex-encoded signature that was calculated from the string to sign and the derived signing key.
Condition: Specify this parameter when you include authentication information in a query string instead of in the HTTP authorization header.
Type: string
Required: Conditional

X-Amz-SignedHeaders Specifies all the HTTP headers that were included as part of the canonical request. For more information about specifying signed headers, see Task 1: Create a Canonical Request For Signature

Version 4 in the * Amazon Web Services General Reference*.
Condition: Specify this parameter when you include authentication information in a query string instead of in the HTTP authorization header.
Type: string
Required: Conditional

AWS Glossary

For the latest AWS terminology, see the AWS Glossary in the *AWS General Reference*.